Aesop's Fables

First published 1983 by
Hamlyn Publishing,
A Division of The Hamlyn Publishing Group Limited,
Bridge House, London Road, Twickenham, Middlesex, England.

Copyright © The Hamlyn Publishing Group Limited 1983

Adapted and published in the United States in 1986 by
Silver Burdett Company, Morristown, New Jersey.

Library of Congress Cataloging-in-Publication Data

Mathias, Robert.
  Aesop's fables.

  Summary: Fifty-nine familiar and not so familiar
fables from Aesop.
  I. Fables. [1. Fables] I. Frankland, David,
ill. II. Rutherford, Meg, ill. III. Aesop. IV.
Title.
PZ8.2.M4A38   1986   398.2'U52   85-25036
ISBN 0-382-09161-2

Printed in Spain

Aesop's Fables

Retold by
Robert Mathias

Color illustrations by
David Frankland

Line illustrations by
Meg Rutherford

Silver Burdett Company
Morristown, New Jersey

Contents

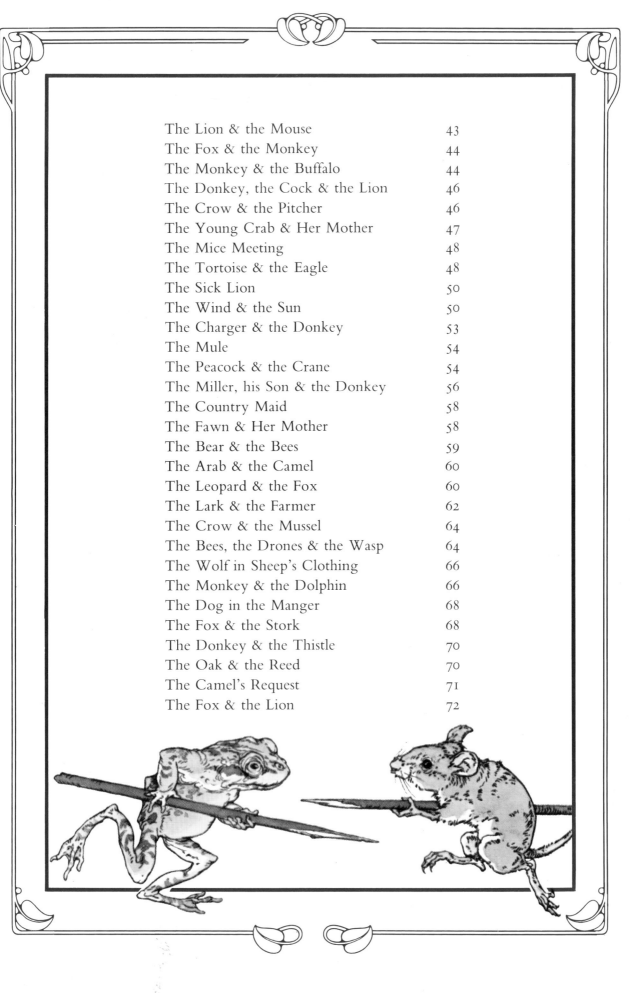

DID Aesop ever really exist? Several legends tell us of a Greek slave called Aesop who lived from about 620 to 560 BC: it is said that he was bought and sold many times, perhaps because of his strange appearance.

He was supposed to have been hunchbacked, with a flat nose, thickened lips and a mishapen head; he also had an unnaturally swarthy complexion. The legends suggest that he suffered from a speech impediment, which must have hampered him when telling tales, though this would not have affected the quick wit of his mind.

Aesop's experiences and travels gave him a knowledge and wisdom beyond that of his fellows. Maybe because of, or in spite of, his disabilities, he had a profound understanding of people and their foibles, which is reflected in the fables. He translated his perceptions into the ways of animals, knowing that in this way it would be easier for people to accept and understand the truth of his simple judgments.

It was Aesop's judgment of people that led, so the legends say, to his death. He traveled to the island of Delphi and declared that from a distance it looked as if it was "of some mighty matter," but when close up, it turned out to be "a heap of weeds and rubbish." His remarks so inflamed the inhabitants that they became angry; they took him and threw him from a high rock and he was killed.

It is likely that in all the legends about Aesop, truth became mixed with hearsay, so it is not known exactly what he did and did not write. Whatever the case, his name and exploits became folklore, with the result that many fables, which he may not have written at all, have been attributed to him.

If Aesop had led a quieter life it might have been a happier one, but for us, that might have meant the loss of perhaps the greatest collection of fables in existence today. Maybe, somewhere, Aesop is quietly smiling to himself as he sees that people have not changed very much from the days when he was telling his tales, two thousand years ago.

The Fox & the Crow

THE cawing of crows filled the air as they swept across the pink sky swooping to and fro in a black cloud towards their untidy homes in the treetops.

They were led by an old and graying bird whose word was law, and behind him came the other older members of the family, who in turn were followed by the younger crows who had been hatched in the spring. These were impatient young birds, proud of their strong young wings and throaty voices. Lagging far behind them, apart from the others, was the most conceited young crow of all.

She had no need to hurry because she was confident that she could easily catch up whenever she wanted. As her wings flapped lazily in the evening sky her bright eyes spotted the open window of a house below her and she decided to investigate.

Swooping past the window she was delighted to see a table in the room beyond laden with delicious food. Turning awkwardly she looped backwards, flew down and through the open window and snatched up a large piece of beef. Her heart beating with excitement, she flew with her prize to a small clump of fir trees standing nearby. The meat was heavy, and breathlessly she settled on a comfortable branch, her bright eyes sparkling with satisfaction and greed.

A dying sunbeam glanced through the branches and settled on something brown and furry among the pine needles and bracken at the foot of the tree. The brown patch moved silently forward and there, in the rays of the setting sun, was a fox.

It was rather early for him to be setting out for his night's hunting, but he was very hungry after sleeping for most of the day. When he looked up and saw the crow with the juicy piece of meat in her mouth his mouth watered with envy.

The crow glanced down at him with scorn. She thought the fox a rather common form of creature. Why, he could not even fly!

DAVID FRANKLAND.

The fox concentrated his gaze upon the meat, his brain working quickly, his amber eyes alive and bright. At all costs, he decided, he must have the meat. His beautiful brush-like tail swayed gently and his tongue flicked over his jaws. Then he smiled up at the crow and said in a soft voice, "What vision of beauty is this that I see?"

The crow cocked her head on one side and stared downward, still holding the piece of meat firmly in her beak.

Then she heard the fox say, "Surely those beautiful wings must have come from a fairy nest, they are so fine and strong! And those eyes, so soft and liquid to behold, so star-like and so gentle . . ."

The crow fidgeted a little and thought, "Perhaps I was mistaken. The fox appears to be a most elegant and sensible fellow."

The fox took a breath and went on: "Never in all my travels have I seen such exquisite poise, such dignity. And such form! Surely even the graceful swans on the lake would be green with envy if they could see such soft and fairy-like lightness!"

The crow preened herself but still held tightly to her prize. She was longing to hear more and waited expectantly. The fox continued, "That smooth beak, those dainty feet. This must be the wonderful crow that I have heard so much about."

The crow took one step to the right and one to the left but still held on to the meat. Then the fox muttered, "Now, if only she could sing like the nightingales! But of course, with such outward beauty she probably cannot sing at all. What a pity!" The fox sighed. "If only she could sing she would be the queen of them all."

The conceited young crow could contain herself no longer. The fox, she decided, was a gentleman of taste and quality. She must show him that her voice was every bit as beautiful as her figure and coloring. She simply could not remain silent any longer, and she opened her beak as wide as possible. "CAW! CAW! CAW!" she croaked, making the most ugly sound that ever was heard.

There was a sudden bark of excitement from the foot of the tree as the slice of juicy meat fell onto the ground. The fox pounced upon it instantly and gripped it between his strong jaws. As he ran off the crow screamed in fury, "CAW! CAW! CAW! You wicked thief! Give me back my meat, CAW! CAW! You wicked thief!" But the fox did not return despite her pleas.

Those who flatter often have an ulterior motive.

The Fox & the Grapes

ALONE fox, long without food and lean with hunger, came to a vineyard after much wandering. The vines were rich with fruit, with many bunches of grapes hanging full and ripe and ready for eating.

As no one was about she stole silently in, but on entering discovered the grapes to be high above her, with the twisting vines strung to a tall trellis, far out of her reach.

She jumped and failed, and jumped again; but her efforts were all in vain. Her tired body began to ache with the repeated attempts to satisfy her hunger. At last, frustrated and angry, the poor fox fell back from her final leap and cried out, "I don't want the grapes anyway, they're sour and not fit for eating."

People pretend to despise the things they cannot have.

DAVID
FRANKLAND.

The Town Mouse & the Country Mouse

ONCE upon a time an honest, sensible country mouse invited his good friend, who lived in the nearby town, to pay him a visit. In due course the invitation was accepted.

The country mouse looked around his humble home, which was just a small hole at the foot of a great oak tree. It was not at all richly furnished but it was comfortable and had, until now, provided for all his needs.

He busied himself tidying up and, although frugal in his nature, generously opened up his heart and his store for his old friend. Each carefully gathered morsel was brought forth from his larder – peas and barley, cheese parings and nuts. All the food he had was piled high to await the arrival of his guest. The country mouse hoped there would be enough to satisfy his friend, whose manners, he suspected, would be dainty. He feared the quality of his food would perhaps not measure up to the delicate palate of a town mouse.

At last the town mouse arrived and, after greeting his friend, they both sat down to eat. The town mouse condescended to pick a bit here and a bit there – he wrinkled his nose and did not seem at all impressed with the fare spread before him. The country mouse ate very sparingly and nibbled busily at an ear of corn. He pretended a lack of appetite in case there might not be enough for his companion.

At length the town mouse sat back and pushed the simple scraps of food disdainfully away from him. "My dear friend," he began, "let me speak frankly with you. How is it that you can endure the dullness of this plain and simple life?" He paused and the country mouse's ears drooped just a little.

"How can you bear," continued the town mouse, casting his eye around the small dark hole where they sat, "to live in such a place as this? You can't really prefer these damp woods to busy streets filled

with carriages and people! Is not the conversation of men more fitting to the ear than the chirping of birds? The warm splendor of a rich house preferable to this wild, windy wasteland?"

The country mouse looked crestfallen. He looked about him and for the first time he saw his humble home as others saw it.

The town mouse puffed up his chest: "You must delay no longer!" he said. "You must leave with me immediately. Remember, we shall not live forever and you cannot possibly waste your life away here."

He stood up and went towards the door. "Come now, I will show you the life of the great town."

Such fine words and so knowing a manner overwhelmed the simple country mouse, and he readily agreed to leave with his friend. Together they set out for the town, waiting when they reached the outskirts. Then, when nightfall closed over the land they sneaked into the city.

It was midnight before they reached the great house where the town mouse lived. Here were couches of crimson velvet, carvings in ivory, everything, in fact, that showed wealth and comfort. On the table were the remains of a splendid meal, and it was now the turn of the town mouse to play the host; he ran to and fro to supply his friend's wants, pressed dish upon dish and tidbit upon tidbit, as though he were waiting on a king.

The country mouse, for his part, tried to appear quite at home, and blessed the good fortune that had brought such a change in his way of life. Then, in the midst of his enjoyment, just as he was wondering how he could have been content with the poor food he was used to at home, the door suddenly opened and a party of ladies and gentlemen entered the room.

The two friends jumped from the table in the greatest fright, and hid themselves in the first corner they could reach. When the room was quiet again they ventured to creep out, but the barking of dogs drove them back in still greater terror than before.

At length, when all the household was asleep, the country mouse stole out from his hiding place, and, bidding his host good-bye, whispered in his ear, "My good friend, this fine mode of living may do for those who like it; but give me barley and bread in peace and security before the tastiest feast where fear and care lie in wait."

A humble life with peace and quiet
is better than a splendid one with danger and risk.

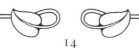

The Dove
& the Ant

T HROUGH the forest ran a clear bubbling stream and under a blade of grass on the bank sat an ant. She felt very thirsty and bent over to take a drink, but as she did so she slipped and fell into the water.

The strong current snatched her away, carrying her far off down the stream. As hard as she tried she could not manage to swim to the bank.

At that moment a dove flew by and, seeing the struggling ant, took pity on her distress. She broke a branch from a nearby tree and dropped it into the water. The ant did not delay but clambered nimbly onto the branch and at last reached the safety of the bank.

Not long after this, the ant was out for a stroll when she came upon the dove again. A hunter was just about to trap the bird with a large net. Seeing what was going to happen, the ant bit sharply into the man's heel and made him cry out in surprise.

The dove heard him, took fright and flew away.

One good turn deserves another.

The Wolf & the Crane

ONE day a wolf came upon a fine fat hen and, thinking this would be an admirable meal, he ate the poor creature to the last feather. Alas for the wolf – with his final mouthful a sharp bone became securely stuck in his throat.

He coughed and spluttered and the tears ran from his eyes, but despite all his efforts he could not dislodge it. In the greatest agony he ran up and down through the woods looking for help.

The wolf begged for relief from each and every animal he met. With each encounter he hinted that a handsome reward would be given if the bone could be removed from his throat. However, his manner was known to many of the animals and they were unwilling to lend him their aid.

The lion and the leopard pretended not to hear his anguished cries; the crow and the raven flapped high into the trees, away from his snarling jaws; the fox and the bear were wary of a trick and went about their business; even the donkey refused to help – at least that's how it seemed, for he merely brayed and continued munching thorns.

At last, as the day drew on, the wolf came upon a crane dipping among the reeds by the waterside. She listened to the wolf's request and, on hearing the promise of a reward, she agreed to help.

Peering deep into the wolf's throat the crane could see the sharp bone stuck fast. Reaching down with her beak and with her long neck curving between the fearsome jaws, she slowly drew it out.

Modestly, the crane asked for the promised reward but the wolf grinned widely, his sharp teeth sparkling in the sunlight. "You ungrateful creature!" he snapped. "Have I not given you your life? How many can place their head in a wolf's jaws and live to tell the tale? Your tasty head has been withdrawn safely, is that not reward enough?"

Those who expect thanks from rascals are often disappointed.

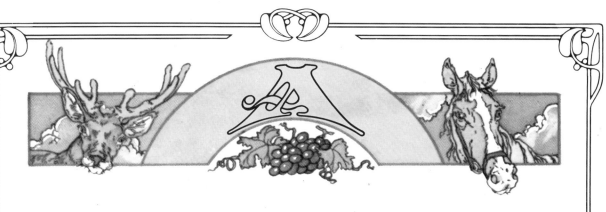

The Horse & the Stag

A LONG time ago a wild horse lived and grazed in a vast green meadow. The meadow was wide and provided the sweetest grass for feeding – no other animal came there and the horse had it all to himself.

One day, much to the dismay of the horse, an antlered stag leaped into the meadow and, trampling around, trod down much of the horse's fine grass. This greatly annoyed the horse and, unable to prevent the stag's destructive behavior, he galloped away toward a man who was passing close by.

"Sir," said the horse, "please stop and help me to punish that intruder before all my grazing land is spoiled."

The man looked back towards the stag who was still leaping about wildly, trampling and stomping; then turning to the horse he said, "Yes, I will help you to be revenged, but first you must let me place a bit in your mouth for a bridle, and a saddle on your back so that I may mount you. I will provide weapons and then, together, we will be able to overpower that willful beast."

The horse agreed eagerly and all was made ready; then with the man mounted on his back he gave chase to the stag. The hunt was short and the stag was soon overcome and slain, which pleased the horse.

He turned to thank the man for his aid but found he could not move his head freely; there was no answer except a sharp tug on the bridle attached to the hard bit in his mouth.

"No need to thank me, horse," said the man, "it is I who should thank you. Until now I did not know how useful you could be, nor how swiftly you could carry me across the land. Your revenge has been rewarding to me for in the future I will keep you as my servant."

Thus from that day to this the horse has been the slave of man.

Revenge is dearly bought at the price of liberty.

The Dog
& the Bone

A WIRY dog, of doubtful reputation, was swaggering home one day when he happened to pass a butcher's shop. Seeing a pile of tasty bones on the counter he greedily snatched one and ran off.

Later, as he went on his way, he crossed a river. Halfway over the bridge he chanced to see his reflection in the water below him. Thinking that it was another dog, and one with an equally tasty meal in its mouth, he resolved to make himself master of the situation.

He growled and snapped at the dog in the water, opening his jaws wide to show off his sharp fangs and so frighten his enemy. Immediately the bone fell from his mouth and plopped into the stream where it sank to the bottom – out of his reach and lost forever.

Be content with what you have.

The Boy Who Cried Wolf

O N a hill above a village stood a young shepherd boy. He was bored and so, to amuse himself, he cried out to the village below: "The wolf! The wolf! The wolf is coming!"

His trick succeeded. Three times the villagers came panting up the steep hillside to help him save his sheep. Each time, when they reached him, the boy just laughed and they felt cheated and angry.

Alas, for the boy, one gray misty day the wolf really did come, and right away the beast attacked the sheep. The boy cried out in earnest: "The wolf is here! Help me! The wolf is here!"

No one answered his call for the villagers thought it just another of his tricks – and the wolf devoured all his sheep.

The boy had learned his lesson too late, that liars are not often believed even when they do tell the truth.

The Hare
& the Tortoise

A HARE met a tortoise one day, and seeing how slowly the tortoise lumbered along, the hare laughed out loud and made much fun of him.

"How slow and clumsy you are," said the hare. "You move so awkwardly in your heavy shell it is a wonder that you ever arrive where you are going."

The tortoise paused on the dusty road and, lifting his head, turned and smiled at the hare. "Then let us have a race together," he said. "At any time you choose – I'll wager five dollars for five miles."

The hare leaped about excitedly. "What, five dollars? Can we start now? Only five miles?" And without waiting for the tortoise to answer he bounded off down the road.

The tortoise set off slowly after him and without looking back, not to the left nor to the right, he made his way steadily and surely along the highway.

Soon the hare's exceeding swiftness put him far ahead and, snickering to himself, he turned to see how far behind the tortoise was. He was nowhere in sight so the hare, feeling a little tired and thinking that a rest would be very pleasant, settled down beside a signpost to take a nap. "I shall sleep for a while," he said. "I've got plenty of time and if my tardy friend the tortoise passes this way while I'm asleep, I will awaken, catch up to him and still win with ease."

Meanwhile, the tortoise plodded on, and after a long, long time he reached the signpost; beneath it the hare was snoring loudly. The tortoise did not stop, he did not even hesitate, but carrying his great shell upon his back he proceeded on towards the distant winning-post.

The hare, fully confident of his victory, slept on in the sunshine. When at last he awakened it was nearly evening: he had overslept! He blinked, leaped up, looked this way and that, and then scampered off as

fast as he could. Although he ran as fast as the wind he failed to catch the tortoise. When he came to the winning-post, the tortoise was already there, quietly smiling to himself.

Slow and steady wins the race.

The Frog & the Ox

AN ox, grazing in a swampy meadow, happened to put his foot on a family of young frogs and crushed most of the unfortunate creatures to death.

However, one escaped and ran off immediately to tell his mother.

"Oh, Mother!" he said, gasping for breath, "while we were playing, such a big four-footed beast trod on us."

"Big?" asked the old frog; "how big? Was it as big" – and she puffed herself out as large as she could – "as big as this?"

"Oh!" said the little one, "a great deal bigger than that."

"Well, was it this big?" and she swelled herself out further still.

"Yes, Mother, it was; and if you were to swell till you burst yourself you would never be half its size."

Annoyed with her little one for doubting her powers, the old frog tried yet again, and this time she puffed so hard that she burst herself in the vain attempt to be what she was not.

People may be ruined by attempting to change the work of Nature.

The Donkey, the Fox & the Lion

THE donkey and the fox entered into partnership together to protect each other, and swore eternal friendship. Soon after, they went hunting, but before they had gone very far a lion crossed their path.

The fox saw the lion first, and, pointing him out to the donkey, said: "We must make terms with this lion and get him to be friendly with us." So saying, he went boldly up to the lion and offered to help him trap the donkey, provided that his own life should be spared. The lion was quite willing to promise this, whereupon the fox induced the donkey to follow him to a deep pit, into which he managed to push him. As soon as the lion saw that the donkey was trapped he sprang upon the fox and made a meal of him. Later he could eat the donkey at his leisure.

Those who betray their friends
must not expect others to keep faith with them.

The Travelers & the Bear

TWO friends were traveling on the same road together when suddenly they came face to face with a large bear.

In great fear, and without a thought about his companion, one man immediately climbed into a tree and hid.

The other, seeing that single-handed he was no match for Bruin the bear, threw himself on the ground and pretended to be dead, for he had heard that a bear will not touch a dead body.

The bear approached him, sniffing at his nose and ears, but the man, with great courage, held his breath and kept still, and at length the bear, thinking him dead, walked slowly away.

When Bruin was well out of sight the first traveler came down from his tree and asked his companion what it was that the bear had said to him. "For," said he, "I observed from my perch that he put his mouth very close to your ear."

"Why," replied the other, "it was no great secret. He wisely advised me not to keep company with those who, when they get into difficulty, leave their friends in the lurch."

Misfortune tests the sincerity of friends.

The Old Hound

A HUNTSMAN long ago had a fine pack of hounds. He had trained them well and they were all skilled in the chase and obedient to his call. One hound, however, stood out among the pack for his exceptional ability and fearless bravery. The master had noted this, and his favor was rewarded by the hound's devotion.

This hound could outrun the stag and the hare; he could outfight the wolf and the fox; he would stand against an enraged bear and bring it down – such was his bravery. Once when his master had fallen from his horse and lay injured, the hound had remained with him all through the dark night until rescue had come – such was his loyalty.

The years passed and, alas, the hound grew old with them. Although he remained as faithful as ever, his speed and skill diminished, his limbs became stiff and his eyes grew tired.

One day, while hunting a wild boar, his master directed him into a wood. With his old legs tired and aching from the chase, the hound plunged through the thicket into the trees. There in a small clearing was the boar, snorting and angrily stamping the ground.

A ferocious battle began; the boar lunged and stabbed with his curling tusks and, although the hound fought back bravely and seized the creature by the ear, he was weakened and tired and could not retain his hold. At last, as his strength ebbed away, he released his grip and allowed the beast to escape.

At that moment his master rode into the thicket and, seeing what had happened, he severely scolded the old hound. He paid no heed to the dog's wounds and would have beaten him there and then had not the hound sadly cried, "Please master, spare your old servant. Although my heart is willing and true, my body is old and feeble. Remember me for what I was rather than for what I am now."

Faithful service should be long remembered.

The Kite, the Frog & the Mouse

THERE was once much argument between a frog and a mouse as to which should be master of the marsh. Both were stubborn and many pitched battles resulted.

The crafty mouse, hiding under the grass, would make sudden attacks upon his enemy, often surprising him at a disadvantage.

The frog was stronger than his rival, however, and, hoping to end the dispute, challenged the mouse to single combat.

The mouse accepted the challenge, and on the appointed day the champions entered the field, each armed with the point of a bulrush. Both confident of success they charged into battle.

A kite chanced to be hovering overhead at the time, and seeing the two silly creatures so intent upon their quarrel, she swooped suddenly down, seized them in her talons, and carried them off as a fine meal for her young.

United we stand, divided we fall.

The Cat & the Fox

A CAT and a fox were exchanging views upon the great difficulties of living in peace and safety from those who were always ready to attack them and take their lives.

"I do not care a bit for any of them," said the fox at last. "Things may be very bad, as you say, but I have a thousand tricks to show my enemies before they can do me harm."

"You are very fortunate," replied the cat. "For my part, I have only one way of evading my enemies should they attack, only one sure method of escape and if that should fail then all is lost."

"I am sorry for you with all my heart," said the fox. "If one could tell a friend from a foe in these difficult times, I would show you one or two of my tricks."

Hardly had he finished speaking when a pack of fierce hounds burst through the trees upon them.

The cat, resorting to her single trick, ran up a tree, and from the security of the topmost branches witnessed the downfall of the conceited fox below her.

Unable to make up his mind which of his thousand tricks he would use to escape, the fox was quickly caught before he could put even one of them into operation.

Pride goes before a fall.

The Birds, the Beasts & the Bat

O NCE upon a time there was a fierce battle between the birds of the air and the beasts of the earth. Alone of all the creatures the bat thought he would remain neutral; he hoped to keep safe and not be harmed by either party.

When the fight began the bat saw that the birds had the advantage and seemed likely to carry the day, so he allied himself with them – but at a distance, the better to see what was going on.

However, the tide of battle began to turn in favor of the beasts. The

bat immediately went over to their side, endeavouring to convince them that he was, by nature, a true beast and would always continue firm and true to their interests.

But once again the fortunes of the battle were reversed, for the eagle led the birds well, and the beasts were soon beaten. In fear the bat now sought only to save his life for he could not bear the shame and disgrace of falling into the hands of his deserted friends, the birds. He ran away – to live alone.

Ever since that fateful day the leathery bat skulks and hides, in caves and holes and musty hollow trees, ashamed to show himself. Only when evening's darkening skies creep down over the earth will he take to the air – when the birds have gone to roost.

You will never win
if you take both sides in a fight.

The Lazy Tortoise

WHEN the great god Jupiter was married he gave a huge feast to which all living creatures were invited. They all arrived early except the tortoise, who came dawdling along just as the feast was about to end.

Jupiter was very angry indeed. "Why are you so late?" he demanded.

"I did not want to leave my home," said the tortoise. "I was quite content and would have been happy to remain there."

Jupiter was angrier than ever to think that his guest preferred a ditch to a splendid palace. "Very well," said he, "if you are so fond of your precious home, you will never again move around without carrying it with you on your back."

And to this day, the tortoise still carries its house on its back.

Laziness finds its own punishment.

The Fox & the Goat

ONE day a fox, who had paused to drink from a well, slipped off the edge and fell into the water. He struggled to climb out, but the steep walled sides were too smooth, nor could he leap from the water to safety. For a long while he pondered on how he could get out again, when suddenly a passing goat, who was feeling thirsty, peered into the well.

Seeing the fox he asked if the water was good and pure, and the wily fox saw his chance to escape. Pretending that he was swimming in the well for pleasure, he replied, "Yes, come down my friend; the water is so nice that I cannot drink enough of it, and," he added, "there is plenty

for both of us.'' The goat immediately jumped into the well and the artful fox, making use of the goat's horns, quickly sprang out.

When the fox was safely on top of the well, he turned and looked down at the goat, who was now splashing about much as the fox had been a moment earlier. He remarked coolly to the poor beast, "If you had as much brains as you have beard, you would have looked before you leaped.''

Think before you act.

The Wolf & the Dog

ONE moonlit night a solitary wolf slipped out from among the shadows. He was lean, half-starved and very hungry. As he loped along he suddenly came upon a very plump, well-fed dog. The two exchanged greetings and the wolf, looking the dog up and down, remarked: "Sir, you do look extremely well. I don't think I've ever seen a more healthy, happy animal. Tell me, how is it that you seem to live much better than I? I may say, without false modesty, that I venture out on the hunt and put my life at risk a hundred times more often than you, yet you are well-fed while I am almost ready to perish with hunger."

The dog grunted. "You may live just as well as I if you choose to do what I do," he said bluntly.

The wolf pricked up his ears. "And what is that?" he asked.

The dog preened, as all those do with secret knowledge: "It's very simple, I guard the house during the night and keep it safe from thieves."

"That I would gladly do with all my heart, for at present I have a sorry time of it," said the wolf. "To change my life in the woods, where I suffer rain, frost and snow, for a warm roof over my head and fine food inside me, would indeed be a bargain." The dog turned and, beckoning the wolf to follow, he set off down the road.

As they jogged along side by side the wolf happened to notice a strange crease around the dog's neck and, his curiosity getting the better of him, he asked its cause. The dog tried to shrug off the question but the wolf pressed him for an answer.

"If you must know," said the dog at last, "I am tied up during the day in case I let my temper loose and bite an innocent stranger – I'm only allowed to roam free at night." He paused and then continued in a tone that seemed to imply that this was the way things should be.

"If I go nowhere during the day, then all I can do is sleep. At night,

when I am turned loose, I am therefore more vigilant. My master and all the family are very fond of me and I am fed with plates of bones and scraps from the table – my reward is considerable, I can tell you."

The wolf stopped in his tracks.

"What is the matter with you?" asked the dog impatiently. "Come along, don't dawdle."

"No," replied the wolf. "Forgive me, but I cannot join you. My liberty is too precious to me and I would not be a king under the terms you describe." So saying the wolf turned and headed back towards the wild woods.

Freedom is better than comfort in captivity.

The Donkey & the Frogs

ONE day, a long time ago, a poor humble donkey was making his way along a track with a load of wood upon his back. Suddenly, rounding a bend in the path, he came to a deep bog and, stumbling clumsily under his load, he slipped straight into it. Despite his frantic struggling, the donkey had the bad luck to sink right up to his neck in the mud amidst a horde of leaping frogs.

"Woe is me!" he groaned and began to bray piteously; then he gave a long sigh as if his heart was about to break in two. The frogs leaped and splashed all round him as he settled deeper into the mire.

"Friend," said one of the frogs to the unhappy donkey, "if you make such a fuss as this simply because you find yourself in a bog, what would you do if you lived here all the time, as we do?"

Custom makes things familiar and easy to us.

The Miser's Gold

A VERY mean man once sold all his goods and property and melted the money he received for it into one solid mass of gold. He took the gold to a forest, where he buried it in the ground. He visited his hoard night and morning to gloat over it.

One night a robber spied on him and when the miser had gone the villain dug up the treasure and went off with it.

Next day the miser missed it and went nearly out of his mind at the loss of his gold. "Why are you making such a noise?" said a neighbor. "You might as well have a stone in the ground instead of your gold, for it was of no use to you when you had it."

Riches are meant to be used.

The Stag & the Pool

ONE summer's day a stag stepped from within a bank of willows and bent to drink from a clear spring. He lapped thirstily and then, as the ringed water grew still again, he paused and saw himself reflected in the pool.

He remained motionless for some time, surveying his shape from head to foot. His dark eyes glowed with pride as he looked at his fine head: "Ah!" he said, "what glorious branching antlers I have! How gracefully they adorn my fine brow, giving such an agreeable turn to my whole face! If only my entire body were so well-proportioned and beautiful then I would hide from no one. But my legs! – I really am ashamed to see them. I know what need we stags have of them and how lost we would be without them, but for my part, I find them so very slender and unsightly that I would rather have none at all."

The stag mused for a while when suddenly his thoughts were shattered by a distant call. Alarmed, he listened intently to the sounds of the approaching huntsmen and the hounds who had tracked his scent. Away he flew in some consternation, bounding over meadow and brush, and leaving the dogs and men a vast distance behind him.

Darting this way and that he ran on. Coming upon a thick wood he plunged, without thinking, into the gloom of the trees. However, ill-fortune struck and he became fast entangled by his horns in a twisted thicket. Tossing his head from side to side he succeeded only in further ensnaring himself. The baying of the hounds drew nearer until eventually they tore him, still struggling, from the thicket.

Knowing what was to happen to him, in the pangs of death, he lifted his head despairingly: "Unhappy creature that I am," he cried, "I realize too late that my antlers, on which I had prided myself, have been the cause of my undoing – and my legs, that I so much despised, were the only thing that could have saved me."

Usefulness is more important than beauty.

34

The Donkey in the Lion's Skin

A DONKEY, of low intelligence, found the skin of a lion. Wrapping it about himself, he set off to frighten all the silly animals he might meet.

Seeing a fox, the donkey approached, and hoping to alarm him he roared aloud. Unfortunately for the donkey, all that came from his throat was a ridiculous braying.

The fox recognized this voice which he had heard before, and he said: "To be sure, I might have been frightened if I had not often heard your foolish bray."

Those who pretend to be what they are not, often give themselves away by overacting.

The Farmer & the Stork

F INDING that cranes were destroying his newly-sown corn, a farmer one evening set a net in his field to catch the destructive birds. When he went to examine the net next morning he found not only a number of cranes but also a stork.

"Release me, good sir, I beseech you," cried the stork, "for I have eaten none of your corn, nor have I done you any harm. I am a poor innocent stork and not like these fellows, as you may see – a most dutiful bird. I honor my father and mother. I——"

But the farmer cut him short. "All this may be true enough, I dare say," he said, reaching for the net. "But I have caught you with those who were destroying my crops, and you must suffer with the company in which you are found."

People are judged by the company they keep.

The Gnat & the Bull

A GNAT, who was very full of importance, buzzed around the head of a grazing bull one summer's day. At length, after much busying and dithering, the gnat settled down on the bull's left horn.

"If," began the gnat, "my weight inconveniences you, my good fellow, please say so and I will be off in half a second."

The bull raised one eyelid sleepily: "Oh, don't bother your poor head about that," he said. "It's all the same to me whether you go or stay – in fact, to tell the truth, until you spoke I didn't even know you were there."

The smaller the mind the greater the conceit.

The Ant & the Grasshopper

O NE dark morning, when the year was not long into winter, the land awoke to find itself chilled by a snow-white frost. All appeared to be still and lifeless beneath the silvery covering, but deep down within the tangled undergrowth, a commonwealth of ants was busily employed. Around and about the winding avenues of their tiny kingdom they managed and turned their corn, exposing it to the air in heaps and so preserving it for sustenance during the cold, cruel days ahead.

As they worked, a grasshopper, who happened to have outlived the summer and was almost starved with cold and hunger, approached them. Shivering, and with great humility, he begged them for a morsel of corn to save his life.

The ants continued with their labors but one of them, sharper than his fellows, turned to the grasshopper and addressed him: "What were you doing this summer?" he asked, his tone less than friendly.

The grasshopper shivered even more – if he had owned a coat he would have drawn it closer around him. "Alas, sir," he whispered, even more humbly, "I passed away the time merrily and pleasantly, in

drinking and singing. I was not idle, or so I thought, but I never once gave a thought to the winter." His voice tailed off plaintively and he sank even lower onto his long frozen legs.

"If that is the case," replied the ant, laughing and shaking up his granary, "all I can say is, that since you sang all summer you may dance all winter."

Save in the good times for the bad times to come.

The Astrologer & the Traveler

A CERTAIN astrologer, who was so interested in gazing at the stars that he forgot to watch his way, had the misfortune to fall into a ditch one dark night. His fellow-traveler, who had been watching the road and not the heavens and was therefore unharmed, said, "Friend, take a lesson from your misfortune and let the stars go quietly on their course in future. It would serve you better if you kept your eyes not on the stars above but on the way you were going."

Look where you're going.

The Cat & the Mice

A CAT who had grown feeble with age, and was no longer able to hunt mice as she had done in her younger days, thought of a way to entice them within reach of her paws.

She suspended herself by the hind legs from a peg, thinking that the mice would mistake her for a bag, or for a dead cat at least, and would then venture to come near her.

An old mouse who had looked on, but was wise enough to keep his distance, whispered to a friend, "Many a bag have I seen in my time, but never one with a cat's head."

"Hang there, good madam," said the other to the cat, "as long as you please, but I will not trust myself within reach of you. *You* are not clever enough for us."

Wise men will not be fooled by old tricks.

The Dog & the Cock

A DOG and a cock were traveling through a wood when night fell. The dog went to sleep in the hollow at the foot of a tree, and the cock roosted in the branches above.

The cock crowed at his usual hour to welcome the dawn, and his cry awoke a fox who lived nearby and who hurried to the tree, thinking he would find himself a meal. When he saw the cock he began to praise his voice and begged the bird to come down from the tree so that he could congratulate him properly.

"I will come down," said the cock, seeing through the fox's plan, "if you will first ask the porter below to open the door."

The fox, not suspecting the trick, did as he was told. When the dog awoke he soon put an end to the fox, and he and the cock journeyed on.

Meet cunning with cunning.

The Lion & the Mouse

ALONG while ago in a country far away there lived a fierce and handsome lion. Once, when weary from hunting and faint from the heat of the day, he returned home to his lair and fell into a deep sleep.

While he slept a small mouse passed by and, not looking where he was going, absent-mindedly wandered into the lion's den. His tiny eyes slowly grew accustomed to the gloom and, as they did so, they opened wider and wider – there, confronting him, was the most fearsome creature he had ever seen. For a brief moment he was rooted to the spot in terror, then in a sudden panic he sprang towards the door. In so doing he stumbled and tripped over the lion's nose and woke him.

The frightened mouse scrambled frantically to pick himself up, but the lion's great paw clapped down upon him. He thought his end had surely come. And it is true the lion would have made a meal of him, there and then, had not the mouse found his voice.

"Spare me, mighty one," he pleaded. "I have accidentally offended you, I know, but your paw is too honorable to stain with the blood of so insignificant a prey."

The great lion looked quizzically at the mouse and considered the matter without speaking. Then, as the mouse lay there trembling, he lifted his paw and allowed his tiny prisoner to go free. Hardly believing his good fortune, the mouse scampered away with hardly a backward look, fleeing as fast as he could out into the forest.

Now it happened that not long afterwards, the lion was once again hunting in the woods and by mischance fell into a trap set by some hunters. He struggled desperately to escape from the net entangling him but to no avail. Angry and with no hope of freedom, he set up a mighty roar that filled the whole forest with its echo.

Far away the mouse heard the roar and ran quickly to discover its source. At last, in a small clearing, he found the captive lion, which he recognized as the same one who had spared his life and set him free. Without more ado, and showing no fear at all, the mouse ran out and began to nibble at the cords that tightly bound the lion. In a short while the mouse's sharp teeth severed the net and the noble beast was released from his captivity.

*Kindness given, to great or humble,
is seldom wasted.*

The Fox
& the Monkey

A MONKEY once danced in an assembly of the beasts, and so greatly pleased them by his performance that they immediately elected him their king.

A fox who envied him the honor, having discovered a piece of meat lying in a trap, led the monkey to the tidbit and said:

"Look! I have found this store, but have not used it. It is not for the subject to lay claim to a treasure trove; the king himself should take it."

The monkey approached carelessly and was caught in the trap, whereupon he accused the fox of leading him into the snare.

The fox replied, "O monkey, can it be that you, with so simple a mind, could rule over all the beasts?"

The simple are easily deceived.

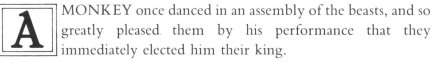

The Monkey & the Buffalo

M ANY years later when the monkey was much wiser he danced again before all the beasts. Once more he greatly pleased them and was loudly applauded. The buffalo, however, was piqued by these attentions and seeking fame himself he stepped forward to dance in front of the animals.

He cavorted and pranced, but his dance was so clumsy and so utterly absurd that all the assembled beasts at first laughed at his foolish antics and then rose up in disgust and drove him out of their sight.

Do not step beyond your abilities.

The Donkey, the Cock & the Lion

ONE day a great lion, feeling very hungry after many hours of fruitless hunting, decided to try and find a meal at a farm. He padded over towards the yard and there, as he expected, was a fine plump donkey, foolishly munching and crunching at a briar.

The lion thought the donkey would make an admirable meal, but perched on a nearby stile was a rangy old cock, and they say that there is nothing a lion hates so much as the crowing of a cock. The lion paused, then he took a step towards the donkey, but at that moment the cock began to crow. The offended lion turned around and bounded off with all possible haste until he could no longer hear the awful noise.

The donkey had idly watched these events and was highly amused at the thought of a lion being frightened by a cock, so he plucked up his courage and galloped after him, delighted to think that he, a mere donkey, was chasing the king of the jungle.

However, the donkey had not followed for long when the lion turned sharply around upon him. The unfortunate donkey never had time to think about his error, and the lion was no longer hungry.

False confidence often leads to disaster.

The Crow & the Pitcher

A POOR crow, who was near to death with thirst, suddenly saw beneath her a water pitcher. Relieved and with great joy she flew swiftly down to it.

However, although the pitcher contained water, its level was so low that no matter how she stooped and strained she was unable to reach it. Thereupon she tried to overturn the pitcher, hoping at least to drink from its spilled contents; but alas, it was too heavy for her.

At length, looking around, she saw some pebbles nearby. Picking them up, one by one, she dropped them into the pitcher. Slowly, by degrees, the water crept up to the very brim and she was at last able to quench her thirst.

Necessity is the mother of invention.

The Young Crab & Her Mother

T HE milky tide hissed and gurgled away from a small rock pool, and two crabs set out for a stroll on the amber sand. "Daughter dear," said the larger of the two, "why don't you learn to walk straight? You are skewing and scuffling and sideways shuffling with every step you take."

"Please, Mother dear," said the smaller of the two, "do but show me how, by your example, and I'll gladly follow your advice."

Practice what you preach.

The Mice Meeting

ONCE upon a time a number of mice called a meeting to decide upon the best means of ridding themselves of a cat that had killed many of their relations.

Various plans were discussed and rejected, until at last a young mouse proposed that a bell should be hung around the tyrant's neck in the future, so that they would have plenty of warning of her movements and therefore time to escape.

The suggestion was received joyfully by nearly all, but an old mouse, who had sat silently listening to the talk for some time, got up and said: "While I consider the plan to be a very clever one, and feel sure that it would prove to be quite successful if carried out, I should like to know which brave mouse is going to put a bell on the cat?"

It is easier to make a suggestion than to carry it out.

The Tortoise & the Eagle

A LONG while ago a tortoise sat on the dusty land and watched the birds wheeling and circling in the air over his head. He grew dissatisfied with his lowly life when he saw so many of them enjoying themselves in the clear blue sky; he longed to join them and share their freedom.

"If only I could get myself up into the air I'm sure I could soar and swoop with the best of them," he thought.

He pondered on this problem for a long time: the sun burned down and he got hotter and hotter and more discontented as he enviously watched the birds.

Suddenly an eagle came to rest on a rock close beside him and, seizing such a favorable opportunity, the tortoise offered all the treasures of the sea if only the monarch of the air would teach him to fly.

The eagle at first declined the task, for he considered it not only absurd but impossible, but, being further pressed by the entreaties and promises of the tortoise, he finally agreed to try.

Taking him up to a great height in the air, the eagle loosed his hold, bidding the stupid tortoise to fly if he could.

Before the misguided creature could express a word of thanks he fell upon a huge rock and was dashed to pieces.

DAVID FRANKLAND.

The over-ambitious often destroy themselves.

The Sick Lion

AN old, old lion realized one day that, thanks to the weakness of age, he was too tired to hunt for his prey any more. Sadly he went home to his den knowing that soon he would die. But before he lay down he stopped at the entrance; breathing with great difficulty and speaking in a slow, low voice he told the world of his sad condition.

The news of the lion's illness soon spread throughout the forest and caused much concern among the other beasts. One by one they came to visit him and pay their respects. However, the lion's age had also made him wily, and as each animal entered his lair and came within reach, they fell an easy prey to the lion, who soon grew fat.

One day, early in the morning, the fox came. He was renowned for his cunning, and approached the den carefully. Standing some distance away he enquired after the lion's health and asked him if he was feeling better.

"Ah, my dearest friend," said the lion, "is it you? I can hardly see you, you are so far away. Come closer, please, and give me some words of consolation for I have not long to live."

The fox, meanwhile, had been looking closely at the ground in front of the lion's den. At last he looked up, and turning to go he remarked: "Bless you, but excuse me if I do not stay, for, to tell the truth, I feel quite uneasy at the many footsteps I see leading into your den yet none do I see emerging."

Think for yourself, and don't follow the crowd.

The Wind & the Sun

LONG ago at the start of the world the wind and the sun were talking together when a dispute arose between them. Which of them was the strongest, they wondered, and to prove the point they agreed to have a contest.

Seeing a passing traveler, they decided to see which of them could

take off his cloak first.

The wind began and blew with all his might, a cold and fierce blast to chill the bone. He tried to blow the man's coat from his back, but the stronger he blew, the closer the traveler gathered his cloak about him and the tighter he clasped it around his throat.

Next, it was the sun's turn: breaking out from behind the clouds he let his warm, welcoming beams fall on to the traveler. The cold and the chill were soon dispersed and the traveler, feeling the gentle warmth on his shoulders, sat down and shrugged his cloak to the ground.

It was clear that the sun had won the contest.

Persuasion is better than force.

DAVID
FRANKLAND.

The Charger
& the Donkey

ONE summer's day a long time ago, a magnificent war horse came along the highway. The charger, adorned with the finest trappings and a great war saddle, was thundering along the stony track, foaming and champing at his bridle. The clattering of his hooves rang and echoed into the crannies and cracks of the mountains, and his loud, shrill neighing was like a peal of battle trumpets.

Presently, the charger came upon a poor donkey trudging slowly and carefully along the same road, laboring under a heavy burden piled high upon his back.

"Get out of my way!" cried the proud horse, his tone haughty and imperious. "Be quick about it, fool, or I'll trample you into the dirt where you belong."

The startled donkey was offended, but not daring to argue with so fine and powerful a beast, he stepped promptly to the side of the road. The charger galloped past, stones flying and sparks crackling beneath his pounding feet. The timid donkey thought the horse made a grand sight as he sped through like the wind. Alone once more, in a cloud of dust, the donkey watched the charger disappear into the distance.

Not long afterwards the war horse was engaged in a great battle, and was blinded in his right eye by an enemy shot. No longer fit for military duties, the once proud horse was stripped of his fine ornaments and tack, and sold to a merchant who harnessed him between the shafts of a heavy wagon.

It was in this forlorn condition that the donkey one day came upon him, painfully tethered to his burden.

"Ah," said the donkey quietly to himself, "I need not have envied him in his pride; if he hadn't been so proud before, I would have been a true friend to him now, helping him and lightening his load."

Pride goes before a fall.

53

The Mule

THERE was once a mule who was as fat as a barrel; she ate too much and she ate too often. She jumped and clopped and kicked about, swishing her tail and exclaiming, "My mother was a racehorse and I'm fine as she."

But, alas, all her weight and self-indulgence got the better of her and she collapsed, exhausted from her frisking. Only then did she remember that her father was a donkey.

There are two sides to every coin.

The Peacock & the Crane

THE peacock preened and strutted, tossing his head this way and that and hardly acknowledging his fellows as he minced along. Suddenly, in the middle of his path, he happened to meet a crane. The crane paid no attention to the conceited bird but quietly continued with his business, dipping and pecking at the scattered seed on the ground.

Drawing himself up to his full height, the peacock looked at the crane with contempt. He displayed his beautiful tail feathers, hoping to shame the creature: "Such a mean, ordinary bird!" he thought.

The crane, however, was not to be slighted quite so easily. He tilted his head to one side and said, "You are indeed a very fine bird, at least your feathers paint you so, but surely it is better to fly high above the clouds on strong wings, than to strut about on the ground like a child's pretty plaything."

Fine feathers do not make fine birds.

54

The Miller, his Son & the Donkey

AMILLER and his son set out one day to take their donkey to a neighboring fair to sell him.

They had not gone far along the road when they met a troop of girls returning from the town, talking and laughing.

"Look there!" cried one of them, pointing towards the two men. "Did you ever see such fools? Fancy trudging along the road on foot, when they might be riding!"

The old man, hearing this remark, quietly bade his son to get on the donkey, and walked along contentedly by the side of him. Presently they came upon a group of old men who were talking together.

"There!" said one of them, "it proves exactly what I was saying. What respect is shown to old age these days? Do you see that idle young rogue riding on the back of the donkey while his old father has to walk?"

"Get down, you good-for-nothing rascal, and let the old man ride and so rest his weary limbs!" cried another.

Upon this the father made his son dismount and got up himself; but they had not proceeded much farther when they met a party of chattering women and children.

"Why, you lazy old fellow!" cried several people at once. "How can you ride upon the beast so selfishly while this poor little lad can hardly keep pace by the side of you?"

The good-natured miller immediately took up his son behind him, and together they rode on the back of the donkey until they had almost reached the town.

"Pray, honest friend," said a townsman, "is that donkey your own?"

"Yes," replied the old man, raising an eyebrow.

"By the way you load him so heavily, one would not have thought so," said the other. "Why, you two fellows are better able and strong enough to carry the poor beast than he you!"

"If you think it the right thing to do," said the old man, "we can but do as you suggest."

So, alighting with his son, they tied the donkey's legs to a stout pole. Lifting it to their shoulders they set off and proceeded to carry him over a bridge that led to the town.

This was so entertaining a sight that the people ran out in crowds to laugh at it, until the donkey, not liking the noise nor the situation,

broke from the cords that bound him and tumbled off the pole into the cold waters of the river below.

Annoyed and ashamed, the old man made his way home again, convinced that by endeavoring to please everybody he had pleased nobody, and lost his donkey in the bargain.

He who tries to please everybody pleases nobody.

The Country Maid

ALONG a country lane stepped a bright young milkmaid, balancing a jug of fine fresh milk on her head. With a fair way still to go to reach the market she started thinking about her future prospects.

"If I sell this milk for a tidy price I can increase my stock of eggs to three hundred. Then, even allowing for those that spoil and those that are stolen by thieves, they should produce at least two hundred and fifty chickens. Then again, just when the price is highest, I will take the birds to market and sell them: I cannot fail to make enough money to buy a new gown. I am so fair and pretty I will look as grand as any lady in the land."

"What color should it be?" she thought. "Shall I buy one in red or green? Yes, green, I think – it suits me best; green it will be! I'll go to the fair where all the fine young men will seek me out for a partner; but I shall refuse them, every one, and dance with a shrug and a toss."

Carried away by her daydream she could not help but toss her head in just such a way as she had imagined. Crash! The jug of milk toppled and smashed on the road in front of her. She watched helplessly as the spilled milk trickled away in the dust, and with it went all of her happy thoughts and dreams.

Don't count your chickens before they're hatched.

The Fawn & Her Mother

WHY is it, Mother," asked the young fawn, "that though you are bigger, and taller, and swifter, and even . . ." her large brown eyes opened wide, "and even," she continued, "have horns to defend yourself, how is it you are so afraid of hounds?"

The little fawn's mother smiled and sighed: "All this, my child, I know full well, but no sooner do I hear the bark of a dog, than for some reason or other, I just cannot stop myself from running off as fast as I can go."

You can't make a coward be courageous.

The Bear
& the Bees

O NE day a bear climbed into an orchard where, beneath the blossoming apple trees, the farmer kept a hive. "Where there's a hive there's bees, and where there's bees there's honey," thought the bear, and started to plunder and pull at the hive to have his sweet fill.

Even though each bee was small, when they gathered together they became a massive army. Setting about to fight off the bear, they swarmed about his snarling head, and though they were not able to pierce his thick skin they each sank their tiny stingers into his ears, his eyes and his nostrils.

The bear grew wild with smarting pain, and struck and swung, clubbed and clawed at the milling throng of bees. His clumsy flailing tore his hide and bruised his head so much that he ran away for safety to nurse far worse wounds than any bees could have given him.

Wrongdoing seldom goes unpunished.

The Arab
& the Camel

AN Arab, having loaded his camel, prepared to set off across the desert, but first he asked the beast whether he preferred to go uphill or downhill.

"Why do you ask me such a question, master?" said the camel dryly. "Is the level way across the plain shut up?"

What use is it to pretend there is a choice when there is none?

The Leopard & the Fox

ONE day a leopard, feeling very proud of his beautiful spots, went so far as to ask himself why even the lion should be thought greater than he, who had so rare a skin. Indeed, so proud did he become that he made up his mind, there and then, to have nothing to do with any of the other beasts of the forest.

This, of course, was soon noticed, and the fox, feeling very hurt and annoyed, went boldly up to the leopard and told him that he was foolish in having such a good opinion of himself.

"You may think yourself very fine with your scattered spots," said Reynard the fox, "but, depend upon it, my friend, people value a bright brain far more than they do a handsome body!"

Beauty is only skin-deep.

The Lark & the Farmer

A BLUE sky covered the countryside and the warm sun was slowly turning the cornfields to gold. In one such field there lived a lark and her family of young chicks. Their nest was hidden beneath the tall shoots and the birds lived there happily.

Above their heads the ripe grain weighed heavily on the bending stalks which swayed in the warm summer breeze. The mother lark, at this time of year, was especially attentive: each day she listened for the sound of the reapers and warned her young family to mind each sight and sound. They should tell her right away if they heard or saw anything strange, for when the reaping was about to start they would have to find a new home.

As the days passed the young larks skittered and dived among the tall grasses surrounding the field, hiding and swooping, one moment in sunshine, the next in shadow. One morning a man's voice interrupted their play and they came close together in a silently listening group.

"It is full time," said the man. It was the farmer and he stood only a pace away from them, feeling the ears of corn between his hard brown fingers. "I must call in the neighbors to help reap my corn," he added.

The youngsters waited until the man had turned away, then they fled to their mother with the news and begged her to take them safely away.

"Time enough, my featherlings," she comforted. "If the farmer trusts to the help of his neighbors he will wait a long time for his harvest." And so saying she settled her chicks under her wing.

A few more days of sunshine passed and the farmer came again, this time standing very close to their nest. Now he was accompanied by his tall and eager son.

"Still nothing done and this corn's ripe and ready," he said. "We cannot depend on our neighbors, we'll call up our uncles and cousins to help."

The young larks trembled once more because he had been so close, but their mother reassured them: "Don't be frightened, the uncles and cousins have fields of their own, so they'll not come, you mark my words." She paused and straightened a feather, then drawing her babes about her she added quietly, "But listen carefully, my chicks, to the next words he says."

The farmer and his son stood in the field again two days later. "'Tis falling, and no one is at work," said the farmer, his face dark with concern. "We must wait for our friends and relations no longer, my lad. We'll sharpen our sickles and reap it ourselves – tomorrow; there's no time to lose!"

The chicks had been listening with bated breath and now they flew to their mother as fast as they could; they cheeped and hopped about excitedly as they waited for her to speak.

"Indeed," she said, "it's time to be off. If the farmer now means to do it himself instead of waiting for others, you may be sure that he will work at it hard until it's done." And without more ado she urged them aloft to seek a new home.

If you want something done then do it yourself.

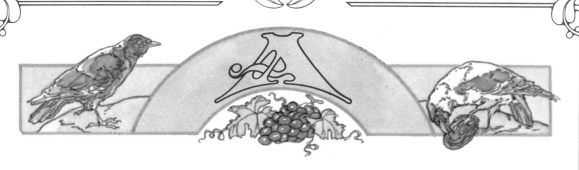

The Crow & the Mussel

ONCE a hungry crow discovered a mussel lying on the seashore and tried hard to break it open with his beak so that he could get at the tasty fish inside. He was struggling without success when a carrion-crow came along and said, "I advise you to use a little strategy, my friend. Carry the mussel into the air as high as you can fly, then, when you let it drop down on this rock, you will find it will break open and its contents will be yours."

The crow thanked him heartily and, thinking it a good plan, flew off, but while he was flying high on the wing the carrion-crow remained on the ground, and ate the mussel himself when it dropped down.

Some people are kind to their neighbors for their own sakes.

The Bees, the Drones & the Wasp

SOME industrious bees discovered a hollow in the trunk of an oak tree, and built a honeycomb in it. Some drones, who lazed nearby and saw a chance of getting a reward without doing any work, at once claimed that they had built it and that it was theirs.

The dispute was unresolved and so the case was brought into court for settlement. Presiding was Judge Wasp, who, being very wise and knowing the habits and character of both parties, addressed them thus:

"The plaintiffs and defendants are so alike in shape and color that it is difficult to say which are the rightful owners. The claims and counter-

claims professed declare a difference of opinion of no small magnitude: it is therefore right and proper that this case has been brought before me." The judge paused and crossed his wings.

"I think," he continued, "that justice will best be served by following a plan which I now propose. Let each party take a hive and build up a new comb, so that from the shape of the cells and the taste of honey it will be quite clear to whom the disputed comb belongs."

The bees readily agreed to the wasp's plan, but the drones, on the other hand, would not do so.

Whereupon the wasp gave judgment: "It is clear now who made the comb, and who cannot make it; this court has no hesitation in giving judgment in favor of the bees."

We may know a tree by its fruit.

The Wolf in Sheep's Clothing

A HUNGRY wolf once found the skin of a sheep, and thought up a cunning plan. He clothed himself in it to cover his color and shape and waited until dark; then he crept stealthily into the sheep-pen amongst the flock.

The foolish sheep, thinking that he was one of their own number, paid no attention to him, and using his disguise he managed to eat quite a few of them before being discovered by the shepherd.

Seizing him, the shepherd slung a rope about the wolf's neck and tied him to a tree which stood close to the pen. He hauled him high.

The next morning some other shepherds passed that way and, seeing what had happened, drew near and expressed their surprise.

"What are you doing?" they said. "Do you hang sheep now?"

"No," replied the shepherd, "but I hang a wolf in the habit and skin of a sheep, when I catch one!" And so saying he pulled aside the skin to show them the dead wolf's body. The others were impressed and applauded him for the justice of his act, for now their flocks would be safe from attack, too.

Appearances can be deceptive.

The Monkey & the Dolphin

A MONKEY sailing on the sea fell overboard and was left far behind by his ship. Just at the moment when he thought he would drown, a dolphin lifted him up from the waves and sped off towards the land.

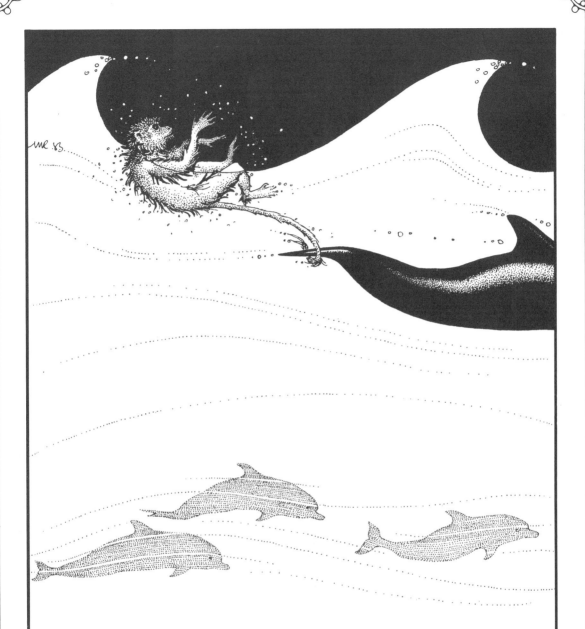

The monkey chattered on his back, relating strange and magic tales, but the dolphin wisely kept his peace and said nothing; until, that is, they neared the coast.

"Do you know this land?" the dolphin asked. The monkey idly nattered on, "Of course! I've been here many times; I know the king and all his court. I am a royal prince, you know!"

The dolphin eyed the barren land where no one lived and no tree stood, then slowly sank beneath the sea to let the monkey swim.

 Your lies will always find you out.

The Dog in the Manger

A DOG once made his bed in a manger, and lay snarling and growling angrily to keep the horses away from their food. "What a miserable cur he is!" said one of the animals to the others. "He cannot eat the corn himself, but he will not let us eat it who can, and are hungry."

Live and let live.

The Fox & the Stork

A FOX one day invited a stork to dinner, and amused himself at the expense of his guest, by providing nothing for him to eat but some thin soup in a shallow dish.

The fox greedily lapped up the soup and it was gone very quickly, while the stork, unable to gain a mouthful with her long, narrow bill, was as hungry at the end of the dinner as when she began.

The fox expressed his regret at seeing her eat so sparingly, and asked, pretending concern, if the dish was not seasoned to her liking.

The stork said little, but she begged that the fox would do her the honor of returning the visit and dining with her the next day, which invitation Reynard the fox readily accepted.

The fox kept the appointment, and, having greeted his hostess politely, he turned his attention to the dinner she had placed before them.

To his dismay Reynard saw that the meal was served in a tall, narrow-necked vessel, and, while the stork was able to thrust in her long bill and easily take her fill, he was obliged to content himself with

licking the outside of the jar.

At last, unable to satisfy his hunger, he retired with as good grace as he could, knowing that he could hardly find fault with his hostess, for she had only paid him back in his own coin.

Those who love practical jokes must be prepared to laugh at themselves.

The Donkey & the Thistle

AT harvesttime the farmer always fed his reapers well. When the sun was high, his donkey was driven into the field. The beast was heavily laden with cheese and ham, fresh-baked bread, good wine and fruit. The reapers ate well and the harvesting progressed quickly.

On the first day a quarter of the field was cut: it would take four days in all and each day at noon the men stopped to eat.

On the last day when nearly all the corn was gathered in and stacked in neat rows, the tired donkey lumbered along under his usual load. He felt not only hot but a little hungry when, there in front of him, he saw a fine large thistle: he stopped and began to munch it contentedly.

It tasted so good that the donkey was moved to think aloud: "So many greedy people would delight at the variety of fare I carry. Yet to me, this bitter, prickly thistle is a savory delicacy that can't be bettered."

Everyone to their own taste.

The Oak & the Reed

ALONE in a meadow there stood a mighty oak tree, at the foot of which there grew a slender reed. One day the wind was blowing strongly, and although the oak remained unbowed, the reed leaned over to the will of the wind, bending and rising with each and every gust.

"Why don't you stand firm, as I do?" asked the oak, and the reed answered quietly, "I have not got your might and power. In fact, I have very little strength at all." The reed bent still lower as the wind blew harder.

"Yes, you are weak," said the oak. "I have so much more strength than you." It had hardly finished speaking when the wind gusted with a renewed force. Tearing at the oak tree, it threw it to the ground, but the reed merely bowed and lifted as before.

The proud will be humbled,
for there is virtue in humility..

The Camel's Request

THE camel approached the Maker of Beasts and coughed and complained about the state he was in.

"Why – oh why," he whined, "haven't I got horns like the bull and the stag? You have given me no weapons at all – no defense!" He sulkily stamped his large feet and knobbled his knees together.

The Maker of Beasts gave a smile. "What an impertinent, silly brute," he thought; then he promptly rejected the camel's request.

"From now on," he said, "you will have shorter ears than those that you have already – let that be a lesson to you, you tiresome beast."

By asking for too much,
one can lose the little that one already has.

The Fox
& the Lion

W HEN a fox who had never seen a lion met one for the first time he was so terrified that he almost died of fright. When he met him the second time, however, he was still afraid, but not quite so much and this time he managed to hide his fear. But when he saw him for the third time he felt so brave that he went up and began to talk to him as though they were old friends.

Familiarity breeds contempt.